Ottawa
A Pictorial Salute

Photo Editor
Richard Vroom

Text
Peter Hopwood

Deneau & Greenberg

Design: Paul Gilbert Design Limited

Canadian Cataloguing in Publication Data

Main entry under title:

Ottawa: a pictorial salute

ISBN 0-88879-022-8 bd.

1. Ottawa, Ont. — Description — Views. I. Vroom,
Richard, 1943- II. Hopwood, Peter, 1928-

FC3096.37.O89   917.13'84044'0222   C80-090022-7
F1059.5.O9088

Ottawa, like many of the world's great cities, was born on water. The confluence of the Gatineau from the north and the Rideau from the south made the Ottawa River at this point the natural junction for commerce of all kinds. First came the **voyageurs**, determined explorers and missionaries like Samuel de Champlain and Jean de Brébeuf, who opened up the river to the Indian trade.

Called the River of the Algonquins at first, it soon became the chief route of the North American fur trade to the northwest and the Mississippi Basin.

The setting for immense flotillas of birch bark canoes laden with gunpowder and rum in one direction and beaver pelts in the other, it also became the scene of violent struggles between rival Indian tribes and their European allies. So vicious were these wars that one tribe, the Huron, were virtually wiped out, and the river was abandoned for many years.

But it was still the shortest route to the west, and was soon re-established as a trade route by a tribe known as the **Outaouais** (trader). It was this tribe who gave their name to the river, the Ottawa. Once again the woods and portages echoed to the shouts and songs of the **voyageurs** and a new breed of rugged entrepreneurs known as **coureurs de bois**.

It wasn't until 1800 that settlement began in earnest in the area. An enterprising and ambitious American from Woburn, Massachusetts, Philemon Wright, looking for a place to establish a small pioneer community, decided to settle on the north side of the river, just below the Chaudière Falls, in what is present day Hull. Wright and his small band of settlers had brought with them the means of forging a life from the land but it wasn't long before their interests turned to lumbering. The vast stands of red and white pine, and the growing market in Britain for Canadian timber offered more lucrative prospects than farming. In 1808 Wright and his men floated the first raft of squared timbers down the Ottawa River to the St. Lawrence and thence to the lumber ships in the harbour at Quebec.

By the year 1818, Wrightstown, as it was called, was a flourishing settlement that could boast a mill, a tannery, a hotel and a distillery — a civilized community was beginning to emerge.

The aftermath of the War of 1812 brought military settlers to the south side of the river, mainly veterans of the Napoleonic wars and their families, who built communities like Perth and Richmond.

The British also decided to build a strategic canal that would form a link between what are now Ottawa and Kingston. For this task they chose Lieutenant-Colonel John By of the Royal Miners and Sappers.

It took Colonel By and his men from 1826 to 1832 to complete the canal and many locks along the hundred and twenty miles of the Rideau River Waterway. At the same time Colonel By planned and built a small community at the head of the canal system where the locks meet the

Ottawa River, near the present location of the Chateau Laurier and Parliament Buildings. The new community was named for its founder — Bytown.

Like Wrightstown across the river, Bytown flourished as a lumber town, attracting entrepreneurs from other parts of Canada and from the United States and Great Britain. These men became known as lumber barons, because of their enormous wealth and power. The major annual event, "the drive," brought timber down on the freshet, the spring flood, from tributaries like the Coulonge and the Madawaska, to be assembled in huge rafts and floated down to Quebec.

The annual drive also brought lumberjacks, **draveurs** and **rafsmen** from the rough austerity of winter camp. These men risked their lives on the log booms and log jams (dozens drowning every year) and were ready for a respite on reaching Bytown. More often than not the respite consisted of women, whisky and wild brawls between rival groups of rivermen. If Bytown became somewhat legendary as a rough and ready lumber town, it also created its own legends — like the strong man and champion of "les canadiens," Joe Montferrand — a real-life Paul Bunyan.

The 1830s and '40s brought shiploads of emigrants from the British Isles, particularly the Irish fleeing the hard times brought on by the potato famines. Many came to Bytown to seek work in the lumber industry as labourers or shantymen. They left their mark, permanently, in the slight Irish twang that visitors sometimes detect in the local Ottawa Valley accent.

After the Act of Union in 1840, which united the two colonies of Upper and Lower Canada (now Ontario and Quebec), it became clear that British North America was moving towards confederation, and that a capital would have to be chosen for the new country. Although not an original candidate for the honour, Ottawa had certain notable advantages. It provided a true, though sometimes turbulent, meeting of the two cultures, French and English — and its setting was spectacular.

The municipal fathers of Bytown decided to change its name to Ottawa in 1853. The name was chosen to commemorate the re-opening of the fur trade by the courageous tribe of the Ottawas two hundred years earlier. In 1857, Queen Victoria chose Ottawa to be the capital of the Dominion that was to be created ten years later.

As a centre of commerce and industry, Ottawa probably reached its peak around 1900. At that time it could claim the largest privately owned business in North America, the J.R. Booth Company — a lumber, paper, railroad and shipping conglomerate that stretched from Georgian Bay in Ontario to Vermont in the United States.

But with the decline of the pine forests and the impact of two world wars, the city took on the calmer demeanour of a stately capital. The burgeoning of government during and after World War II brought a new era of prosperity.

Though now largely a government town, Ottawa is also home for small industry and many national organizations. The city has doubled in population since the war years and spawned several satellite communities as well. Its two languages add a certain flavour of cosmopolitanism rare in a city of its relatively small size. Ottawa has made immense strides as a centre for recreational and leisure activities. Its hills, parkways and waterways provide the perfect backdrop for joggers, cyclists, sailors and campers in the summer; and skaters and skiers in the winter.

Altogether a great place.

Left, Samuel de Champlain, Nepean Point
Above, Lieutenant-Colonel John By, Major's Hill

The Parliament Buildings with
their buttresses and spires
retain the gothic majesty
inspired by the mother of
parliaments in Great Britain.
The original Centre Block of
Parliament was destroyed by
fire in 1916, but the magni-
ficent library behind was saved.
Parliament Hill was once
known as Barracks Hill when
Colonel By and his men used it
as a bivouac.

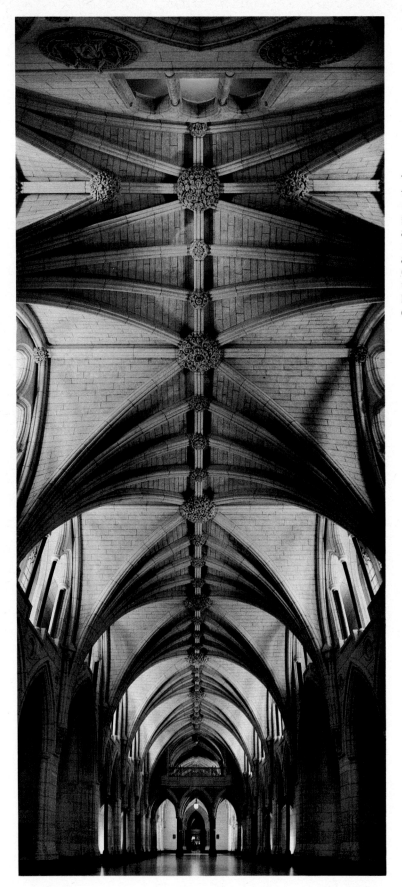

The Hall of Honour, leading from the entrance to Parliament, an impressive introduction to the history and heritage of Canada. Embodied in its carved figures and emblems is the spirit of Confederation and its sense of unity in diversity. Much carving has yet to be done as the country's destiny unfolds.

The Opening of Parliament provides the ritual
and ceremony often associated with the British
tradition. This is the occasion on which the
Governor General (or the monarch) reads the
Speech from the Throne to the joint session of
the Commons and Senate.

The Langevin block (above) with its Renaissance revival facade houses one of the offices of the prime minister. The foyer of the Supreme Court building (right), appropriately magisterial as befits the nation's highest court. The incomparable rib-vaulted dome and cupola of the Library of Parliament (far right), considered to be the best example of neo-Gothic design in the world.

Ottawa is rich in statuary. The scene above is part
of the National War Memorial, unveiled by King
George VI in 1939 to commemorate the
Canadian dead in World War I. The figures, which
suggest heroism and self sacrifice, represent
the various branches of the services.

Many sculptures adorn the precincts of Parliament. Gargoyles and lions, according to tradition, protect buildings from evil or harm.

Left, is Henry Albert Harper, as Sir Galahad. A reminder of the many past tragedies in the rivers of Ottawa, he died trying to save a girl from drowning.

Rideau Hall (left) is the official residence of the Queen or the Queen's representative, the Governor General. It was built by Ottawa businessman Thomas MacKay in 1838. The royal armorial bearings in the frieze are a striking feature of its exterior.

Footguards are the high stepping busbied sentries on duty in the summer at Rideau Hall. Earnscliffe, residence of the British High Commissioner to Ottawa, was the home of Canada's first prime minister, Sir John A. Macdonald from 1883 to 1891. It was Sir John who suggested the name (eagle's rest).

The scarlet and blue of the Royal Canadian Mounted Police add an element of dash to the pomp and circumstance that is part of a capital city. Their world famous musical ride (left) is reminiscent of an era when fine horsemanship and discipline were the essentials of a frontier force. Below, the most popular event in the city during the summer months is the changing of the guard on Parliament Hill.

Canada Day celebrations on July 1st bring out
Ottawans and visitors in their thousands.
Professional entertainers and dancers provide
a variety of acts that reflect the richness of
Canada's cultural heritage.

The long summer nights in Ottawa offer a multitude of enjoyments. Below, a concert in the Astrolabe Theatre on Nepean Point, where the statue of Samuel de Champlain surveys the route upriver.

The National Arts Centre on
Confederation Square provides
a focus for much of the city's
cultural life, and an elegant
modernity to an older area.

When the National Arts Centre opened in 1969 it was one of the most up-to-date theatre complexes in the world. It still ranks among the great theatre houses of the world. Its decorative curtain was woven in Japan.

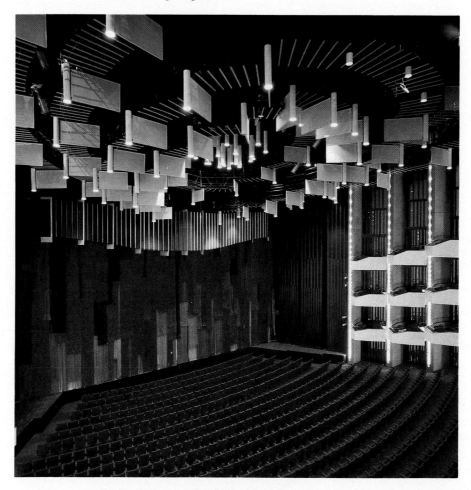

The National Arts Centre is the home of the internationally applauded NAC Orchestra, under the artistic direction of the equally acclaimed Mario Bernardi. As well as founding this excellent orchestra, Maestro Bernardi has also organized one of North America's best known music festivals. The summer festival makes the city a mecca for opera and chamber music lovers during the summer period.

When John By built his canal and locks at the entrance to the Ottawa River, he could not have imagined the amount of enjoyment his military masterpiece was going to bring future generations. As a haven for small boats, and a byway for the casual walker, it is unequalled. The Chateau Laurier hotel lends an exotic but peaceful flavour.

26

Buldings tell a story. Far left, the modern head office of Bell Canada towers above Grant House, named for Sir James Grant, physician to governors general, who built the house in 1875. Formerly the University Club, it now houses a restaurant. The group here reflects the various styles of architecture in the city. From top left, clockwise: the convex curve of the Public Service Alliance Building on Gilmour Street; the Wedgewood Building, considered a marvel when it was built for its bay windows and Italianate style — and its elevator, the first in the city; the Transportation Building on the corner of Rideau Street and Sussex Drive, which once housed City Hall and, later, the National Capital Commission; the new Ottawa Public Library with its cool angularity; and the post office building on Sparks Street, built in 1939, and designed to blend in with the "parliamentary" style.

(Preceding page) The downtown centre is a blend of the elegant past and inventive present. The reflecting glass facades of the Bank of Canada bulding give the looking glass effect of space within space to the juncture of Bank and Sparks streets. The round-topped building behind is the revolving restaurant of the Holiday Inn.

The outdoor cafe has become a popular feature of Ottawa life in the summer months, giving the city a European flavour. The Sparks Street Mall combines the bustle of summer shoppers with the more relaxed boulevard and cafe atmosphere.

Spring has always been a special time in Ottawa. No longer the scene of the timber drive and log booms, it is now the season of crocuses and daffodils on Parliament Hill. The banks of tulips along the driveways bring thousands of tourists to Ottawa in May. They were originally the gift of Queen Juliana of the Netherlands, who lived here during the Second World War, for Canada's generosity and sacrifice.

There are many spots along
Ottawa's parkways where
the walker or cyclist can find
a quiet respite. Ottawa's many
parks and benches make it an
ideal city for the traveller on
foot.

The view from the south of the city takes in the canal to the left, the Rideau River to the right and Colonel By's artificial lake, formerly called Dow's Great Swamp. To the left of the canal is the arboretum of the Experimental Farm. In the centre is one of Ottawa's several important educational centres, Carleton University.

Not many cities have the advantage of a thousand acres of open space in their centre. Ottawa is fortunate — the Central Experimental Farm provides an oasis of flowers, open pastures and trees. It also houses the Dominion Observatory with its fifteen inch reflecting telescope.

As the capital city, Ottawa is blessed with Canada's national museums and art gallery. The National Museum of Man and the National Museum of Natural Sciences are both housed in the Victoria Memorial Building, a castle-like structure at the bottom of Elgin Street. The Museum of Man displays much of Canada's native heritage in its exhibits, such as these Indian ritual masks. The Natural Sciences Museum offers a step back to pre-human times when dinosaurs roamed the primeval forests of what is now the Prairies.

Some of the better known
attractions of the city.
Below. Gold in the vaults of
the Royal Canadian Mint.

Above. Restoration work in the National Gallery,
which houses a fine European and Canadian
collection.

Right. An ancient horse-drawn fire engine from
the Museum of Science and Technology, a great
place for kids and curious adults who like to
touch exhibits as well as look at them.

Below. Laurier House. The
former residence of prime
ministers Sir Wilfrid Laurier and
William Lyon Mackenzie King,
the house is now a museum.

Churches and schools were important landmarks
in early Canada. The Basilica of Notre Dame is
the oldest and perhaps the finest example of
church architecture in the city. It is also a place
of pilgrimage, being the depository for the
remains of two saints, St. Victor and St. Felicity.
Beside the Basilica is the former Collège de
Bytown, an early institute of higher learning,
later to become the Academie de la Salle where
many French-speaking Ottawans earned their
early education.

The Byward Market has been in business for over a hundred years. It is part of the life of Lower Town, where a kind of melting pot of Scottish, French, English and Jewish lived and fought and flourished for a century. Once a somewhat rundown area, it has now become the chic place to shop, eat and be entertained.

Yet another historic landmark in the region is the typical French Canadian church of St. Francois de Sales at Gatineau Point. This pretty church with its sky-piercing spire often attracts sketchers and painters. The log booms still seen on the Gatineau and Ottawa rivers remind us of the once hardy and dangerous living earned on the region's rivers.

A drive out on one of Ottawa's parkways can also be a journey back into the past. Many of the outlying towns and villages have picturesque buildings — like the Mill of Kintail, near Almonte, Ontario.

Not far from the city, the Gatineau Hills offer a vast scenic and recreation area, with trails, drives and camping grounds. They have traditionally been the summer getaway area for Ottawans, a land of lakes, gentle hills and cottages. Former Prime Minister Mackenzie King donated his estate, Moorside, at Kingsmere, to the nation. He was a collector of stonework in his travels abroad; called the Ruins, his collection adds a bizarre element to the rural setting.

One way of travelling up the Gatineau is to take the steam train from the Museum of Science and Technology to Wakefield, Quebec, a pretty town in the hills. The train, popular with visitors and tourists, makes the journey regularly during the summer.

Ottawa is without peer as a place for outdoor and sporting activity. It is often host city for major events like marathons, regattas and bicycle races. For sailors, the waters of the region provide ideal opportunities for courting the wind.

A canal has many uses. In winter it serves Ottawa as the world's longest skating rink, five miles of ice from the National Arts Centre to Hart-well's locks opposite Carleton University.

Winter offers many varieties of recreation in and around Ottawa. Not only is there ample room for skaters and skiers but even for the dog-sledders, who come for the winter carnival to test their skills and the endurance of their animals.

Though winter muffles the sounds of summer, the boom of the Noon Day Gun on Major's Hill gives a sense of the city's continuity and its past. The gun, a souvenir of the Crimean War, has sounded the lunch hour in the mills and offices of the town for over a century. Not far away, Ottawa's City Hall presides over a frozen Rideau Falls that once powered early mills and which so impressed Samuel de Champlain, when he first discovered them. In a sense, he also discovered a splendid community.

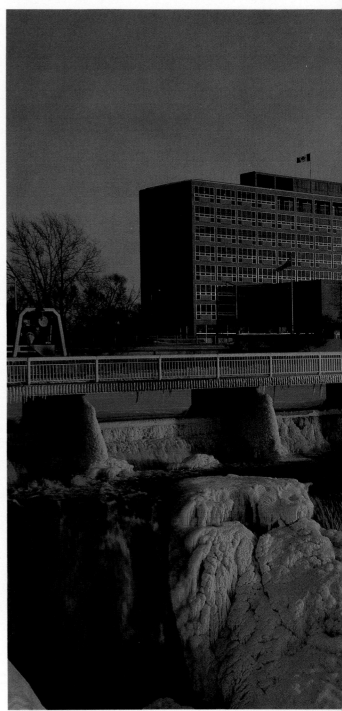

The publishers wish to acknowledge the help of the agencies and organizations that put their photographs at our disposal: Canadian Government Office of Tourism, Miller Services, National Capital Commission, National Film Board of Canada Photothèque.

Photographers: Bob Anderson, Hans Blohm, Harold Clark, Bryce Flynn, Ted Grant, Chris Lund, Malak, W.J. Marsh, Larry MacDougal, Hugh MacKenzie, Crombie McNeill, Tim O'Lett, Otto, Ron Poling, Richter, Helmut Schade, Diana Thorpe, John de Visser, Richard Vroom, Daniel Weiner, Jim Merrithew, photo researcher.

Photo Credits: 1 Malak; 4 Colour Library International, Miller Services; 5 Bryce Flynn; 6,7 Richard Vroom; 8 Richard Vroom; 9 Richard Vroom; 10 Chris Lund, NFB Photothèque; 11 Ron Poling; 12 Richter, NCC (left), Ted Grant (right); 13 Richard Vroom; 14 Richard Vroom; 15 John de Visser (top six), Richard Vroom (bottom); 16 Malak; 17 Richter, NCC; 18 Daniel Weiner (top), Diana Thorpe (bottom); 19 Malak; 20 Richter, NCC; 21 Malak; 22 Harold Clark; 23 Malak; 24 Richter, NCC; 25 Bob Anderson, CGOT; 26 Malak; 27 Helmut Schade; 28,29 Malak; 30 Helmut Schade; 31 Helmut Schade; 32 Richard Vroom; 33 Malak; 34 Malak; 35 Malak; 36 John de Visser; 37 Ron Poling; 38,39 Malak; 40 Richard Vroom; 41 Ted Grant (top), Malak (bottom); 42 Richter, NCC; 43 Otto, Miller Services; 44 Malak (top left), John de Visser (bottom left), Crombie McNeill (right); 45 Richter, NCC; 46 Helmut Schade; 47 Malak; 48 Hugh MacKenzie; 49 Richard Vroom; 50 Malak; 51 Richard Vroom; 52 Richard Vroom; 53 Richard Vroom; 54 Richard Vroom; 55 Richter, NCC; 56 Crombie McNeill; 57 Richard Vroom; 58 Larry MacDougal; 59 W.J. Marsh (top left), Richard Vroom (top right), Malak (bottom); 60 Richter, NCC; 61 Richard Vroom (top), Tim O'Lett (bottom); 62,63 Malak; 64 Blohm, Miller Services.